HOW MIGHT I?

Applying design thinking to transform individual lives

Ramanathan J

Copyright © 2019 by Ramanathan J. All Rights Reserved.

All rights reserved. No part of this book may be reproduced in any form or by any electronic or mechanical means including information storage and retrieval systems, without permission in writing from the author. The only exception is by a reviewer, who may quote short excerpts in a review.

Cover designed by Ramanathan J

CONTENTS

Introduction: 2
Overcoming constraints 11
Defining design thinking 16
Stages of Individual Transformation Exercise 23
Conclusion 46

INTRODUCTION:

Design thinking is a popular methodology among management and leadership teams in corporations around the world. Companies use design thinking to come up with new products and services for their customers. Famous design thinking consultancies such as IDEO work with their clients to brainstorm, innovate and develop new solutions.

Some of the key principles for design thinking include human-centricity and a deep understanding of customer's needs. Hence, many products or services resulting from applying a design thinking process greatly appeals to a customer.

However, design thinking need not be restricted to business process, product and service innovation. We can use this approach for transforming aspects of individual lives as well.

This transformation could mean anything depending upon the individual whom you ask. For instance, a young adult might be overweight and for him reducing obesity and improving fitness levels could mean a significant change. For another woman, physical fitness may not be an issue but she might be suffering from social anxiety which in turn hampers her ability to network, socialize and eventually forge great relationships.

Once we consider an individual transformation challenge to be equivalent to a corporate innovation requirement, we can apply principles of design thinking to achieve enduring change. This text is an attempt to uncover the process of applying design thinking methodology for achieving individual objectives.

I have tried to break down the seemingly holistic and creative endeavor of design thinking into couple of discrete stages. Each stage or phase would be crucial in exploring rich information that can be used for our individual goal setting and change exercise.

The process of analyzing and mapping key data in each of these stages is in itself a rewarding exercise that would empower individuals towards greater levels of self-awareness. I have also incorporated a fictitious case study of an corporate manager named John D, who is trying to overcome his obesity issue and achieve greater fitness levels.

Constraints

We have seen numerous personal coaching and transformation books that brand themselves as a magic pill solution towards achieving individual goals. However, the real process of individual transformation is rarely effortless in nature. We as human beings have set of constraints that we must be aware of before embarking on an individual goal setting exercise.

Starting an individual transformation process by sidelining or ignoring these constraints would be similar to bringing a knife to a gunfight. Hence, following are the limitations that any average human being would face while trying to accomplish a multiple phase project of individual or commercial nature.

Energy

Human beings have finite reserves of energy to carry out daily tasks. We might think that we can utilize our seemingly limitless willpower and power through a list of activities on any day. However, we are applying our cognitive faculties to complete simple or complex tasks. Hence, we are constantly using our conscious energy from the moment we wake up. We need to be mindful of our own energy levels and plan our individual transformation exercise accordingly.

The following example will emphasize the importance of energy in an individual goal accomplishment exercise. Let's assume you have to solve a complex crossword puzzle. There are many ways that you can use to approach this crossword puzzle. You can attempt to solve the crossword in the morning immediately after you wake up. Or you can play a grueling game of chess with your friend and then attempt to solve the crossword puzzle.

Now, can you guess in which case you will be in a far better position to solve the crossword? You will be in a good position to solve the crossword when you have an abundant reserve of conscious energy at your disposal. Hence, you can quickly solve the crossword when you approach it in the morning immediately after you wake up. However, your cognitive faculties and energy levels are significantly dissipated after you play a difficult game of chess. This makes it more challenging for you to solve the crossword puzzle subsequently.

Thus, we need to obtain a certain degree of capability for planning and monitoring our schedule as well as energy levels. This would enable us to accomplish our goals related to design thinking based individual transformation exercise easily.

Morale

What is the most precious asset of any army fighting a war? It is not superior weapons or number of fighting personnel. The answer is morale. Throughout history, military generals and leaders have ensured that the morale of their army remains high irrespective of the setbacks faced in various battles.

An army fighting with low morale will simply stop following its leader's commands and would either surrender or will retreat from the battlefield. On the other hand, an army with a very high morale will simply brush off the attrition or setbacks that it faces in a battle as temporary and would come up with superior strategies and tactics to win the war.

Accomplishing objectives related to an individual transformation exercise is nothing less than fighting a personal war. Those who intend to apply design thinking based methodology for achieving individual goals must be willing to wage a daily battle against procrastination, entrenched behavioral patterns and disillusionment.

Completing even the smallest of daily tasks, identified as a part of the overall transformation exercise, would be immensely helpful in maintaining a high morale and a positive attitude towards completing the individual transformation exercise.

Momentum

HOW MIGHT I?

When we set out to accomplish any task, sometimes we are able to plan and complete our activities effortlessly. In such cases, we are able to achieve a high level of efficiency and effectiveness. In other instances, we seem to face an invisible obstacle while trying to plan and complete the simplest of tasks. As a result, our efficiency levels in such cases drop significantly.

What could explain the difference in the ability to complete goals in both instances? Cognitive energy levels could be one reason. Like we saw in the case of solving crossword puzzle, when we chose to solve the puzzle makes a difference in our ability to quickly obtain a solution. However, another important factor that is crucial in determining our ability to accomplish any activity is the extent of inner momentum that we have towards that activity.

For example, let us assume that we are trying to learn a foreign language. Now, if we are able to create and follow a routine in which we learn at least one or two new words daily as well as practice the pronunciation of the words learned a day earlier, we would be able to quickly grasp the basics of the foreign language and soon we will be able to advance to the next stage of learning complex grammar and words.

On the other hand, if we learn 10 new words on one day and then come back to learn the language after one month, we would be unable to assimilate the concepts perfectly. Our ability to learn this new language is hampered by a lack of inner momentum.
Like in the case of morale, we must maintain our inner momentum by striving to complete at least one small task related to our individual transformation exercise.

We may have planned to complete 5 tasks related to individual transformation exercise in a day but even if we are able to accomplish one small task by the end of the day, we would have maintained our inner momentum.

This inner momentum would play a decisive role in our ability to successfully accomplish the overall objectives of the inner transformation exercise.

OVERCOMING CONSTRAINTS

Following are some of the techniques that you can follow in order to overcome the constraints listed earlier. You can use these techniques as a springboard to prepare a suitable protocol or schedule for planning and accomplishing an individual transformation exercise.

Ensure one uninterrupted block of time for planning and analysis

Ensure that you obtain one uninterrupted block of time when you can analyze and plan activities for the individual transformation exercise. Identify an hour or two in a day and disable notifications in your smartphones or put them in silent mode during this time period. Switch off television and the internet in your laptop and focus on your planning and analysis for the transformation exercise. Note down the ideas and insights that you obtain during the analysis in this block of time.

You will immensely benefit from being free of distractions and interruptions during the thinking and planning time. You will not be required to switch your attention from thinking about your task to responding to the notification on your phone. You can write down your points or ideas related to the exercise and need not be focused on the email or a news website that is open in another tab of your internet browser. The quality of your ideas and the speed with which you will come up with these ideas would be significantly higher if you can dedicate a single uninterrupted block of time for planning and analysis.

Create and sustain an activity streak

HOW MIGHT I?

An activity streak implies a task that is performed daily for a series of days. For example, if you go to a gym and workout for one hour daily for 6 days, then you have an activity streak of 6 days. If you are unable to go to gym on the 7th day, then your activity streak is broken and your previous activity streak will remain at 6 days.

You would want to obtain an activity streak with longer duration because in that case, your inner momentum will be sustained and you will be able to accomplish your daily tasks with relative ease. This in turn will benefit you towards achieving the overall goals of the individual transformation exercise.

Obtain feedback in regular intervals during the transformation exercise

Imagine that you are playing a game of tennis and there is no scoreboard to track the match score. You will be unable to know who is winning or losing the match. Feedback in a transformation exercise is like a scoreboard. Feedback gives you the information about the overall progress that you have made towards accomplishing the objectives of the transformation exercise.

You can obtain feedback during key stages of the transformation exercise. For example, if your individual transformation goal is to reduce weight in a specific time period, then your feedback could be the exact weight at various milestones or phases during the entire duration of the exercise.

If your goal is to improve your socializing and networking skills, then your feedback could be the number of new social contacts that you have established or the number of networking events that you have participated in two weeks. You can decide the duration or the extent before you arrive at a milestone or before you complete a phase. You can define each phase to be of two weeks, one week or even a month as per the outcome of your planning and analysis before starting the entire exercise.

HOW MIGHT I?

Hence, if you conclude that measurable progress or feedback for a weight reduction transformation exercise cannot be attained in a week, then you can define the duration of a phase for such an exercise at two weeks or even a month.

DEFINING DESIGN THINKING

Before we examine further the process behind design thinking based individual transformation exercise, we need to understand what design thinking itself is all about. Some of us who hear the term design thinking for the first time may think that this term probably relates to creative professionals or artists. However, the term design thinking has broader connotations and has far ranging applications across various commercial disciplines.

I would like to define design thinking in the form of a three layered pyramid as follows:

HOW MIGHT I?

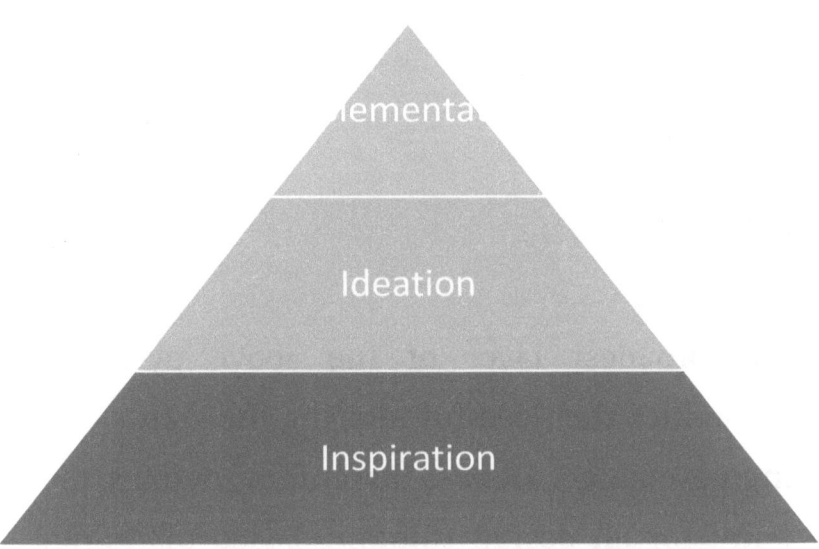

Pyramid representing Design Thinking methodology

Inspiration

This is the broadest layer of the above pyramid. Inspiration defines the need for altering the status quo or for bringing change. Hence, inspiration defines the starting point for all design thinking based planning, analysis and implementation.

In case of companies, inspiration or need for bringing change could be the result of increased competition, introduction of new technology, need to enter new markets or strengthening current market dominance.

In case of individuals like John D, our corporate manager who was introduced in the case study description earlier, inspiration or the need to change status quo could result from his awareness of how his obesity issue and poor fitness level is affecting his ability to be more productive at work. This self-awareness in John could inspire him to seek a plan for bringing change.

Rich data can be generated in the inspiration stage of design thinking process. This data need not be only numbers or tabular data. Instead, this data could also be observations, recorded feelings or thoughts. This data forms the basis for further stages of the design thinking process.

Ideation

Data generated from the inspiration stage can be analyzed in the next stage known as ideation. In this stage, we try to uncover the underlying patterns in the data. We use these insights to form ideas for the subsequent stages. Ideas generated in this stage identifies the key areas where we need to focus our resources. The ideas could also give a broad theme of exact tasks that we have to accomplish in the subsequent stage.

Implementation

Inspiration and ideation stages lay the groundwork for the design thinking phase known as implementation where we put the ideas to practice. Unless we use the ideas to come up with tasks that we can try to accomplish, the entire design thinking process could end up becoming just an academic exercise.

Implementing the ideas would allow us to obtain vital feedback about the complete design thinking process. This feedback would enable us to make course corrections and alter our plans as well tasks for improving the overall effectiveness. Implementing ideas would also enable us to monitor the results at various milestones.

In case of John, he could come up with several ideas for reducing his weight and improving his fitness levels. These ideas could include going to gym and work out for an hour daily, eat an organic diet, stop watching television and instead join a local club for learning tennis and so on. John can try all or some of these ideas and observe the results.

John can decide when he would call a milestone and monitor results. For instance, he might go to gym daily for a month and then check his weight at the start of the next month. Or he may follow a complete organic diet for two weeks and then check his weight on the day 15.

Similarly, you can experiment with creating your own tasks and defining your own milestones based on what works best for you. You can do an pilot or initial testing of tasks and milestones and check whether you are able to feel or observe noticeable change towards achieving the overall objectives of the exercise. For example, you might want to improve your socializing and networking skills.

Subsequently, you can define the tasks to be the number of trade conferences or networking events that you attend and the number of new acquaintances that you make in a week. Thus, the milestone in this case is a week. You can monitor your progress at the end of every week.

STAGES OF INDIVIDUAL TRANSFORMATION EXERCISE

I have tried to build on the earlier mentioned concept of three layered pyramid representing the design thinking process in order to create a more practical series of steps that can be applied for any individual transformation exercise. I would like to call this process as 5S-ITE or the five steps of individual transformation exercise.

5S-ITE can be followed in a sequential manner so that every subsequent step builds on the data or insights obtained from the previous steps. Recording observations, analyzing data, extracting insights, verifying feedback and altering tasks or components of the overall plan is an inherent part of the exercise.

This is similar to the way an artist uses his brush and colors over an empty canvas. The artist tries brushes of different strokes as well as colors of various hues and shades during the course of painting his vision on the canvas. As he experiments with these colors, he sees the overall painting gradually unfolding in front of him.

Similarly, observation and acting upon feedback is an integral part of 5S-ITE at various stages. For instance, you may complete a task and then observe the results. You may realize that some of your underlying assumptions while defining the particular task did not match the actual results. Hence, you may have to rethink the entire task as well as the schedule as required.

HOW MIGHT I?

However, as you keep on applying the principle of observation and acting upon feedback across various stages of the 5S-ITE process, you will be able to define tasks and schedule with a greater precision.

This is because gradually, you will be able to better understand your own constraints as well as the multitude of factors that are in play when you try to achieve your individual transformation goal. Your ability to work around your constraints will improve significantly as well.

5S-ITE Stages

Following are the individual stages of the 5S-ITE process.

1. Persona Mindmap

Persona mindmap is a derivation of the immensely popular brainstorming technique called as mind mapping. Mind mapping is a visual and creative way of representing central and secondary ideas related to any topic or context. A mind map is a visual thinking tool that can be applied to cognitive functions such as learning, creativity or analysis.

A mind map depicts thoughts using keywords that trigger associations which in turn triggers further ideas. The primary idea in any mindmap is placed in the center of the diagram. The secondary or complementary ideas related to the central idea are represented as branches emerging from this primary idea. Subsequent branches can also be drawn in order to make the mindmap more expansive or detailed.

Persona mindmap is similar to generic mindmap. However, in case of persona mindmap, the central idea is related to the person or the individual. We identify the attributes, behavioral patterns, likes or dislikes, motivations, social relationships and so on in the persona mindmap.

The reason we create a persona mindmap is because an individual is at the core of 5S-ITE or the individual transformation exercise. All the goals, planning, tasks and feedback is designed in order to achieve individual transformation. Hence, we need to understand the various dynamics that influence a person before we set out to complete the five stages of individual transformation exercise.

We can use various software or free online tools to draw a mindmap. However, we can simply use paper and a variety of color pens to draw a mindmap. We would be able to think more creatively when we use paper and color pens with our hands as compared to using a software or an online tool.

We can also try to take words, headlines or pictures from newspapers and magazines and paste them to the various ideas in the mindmap drawn on paper in order to increase the overall visual appeal of the mindmap.

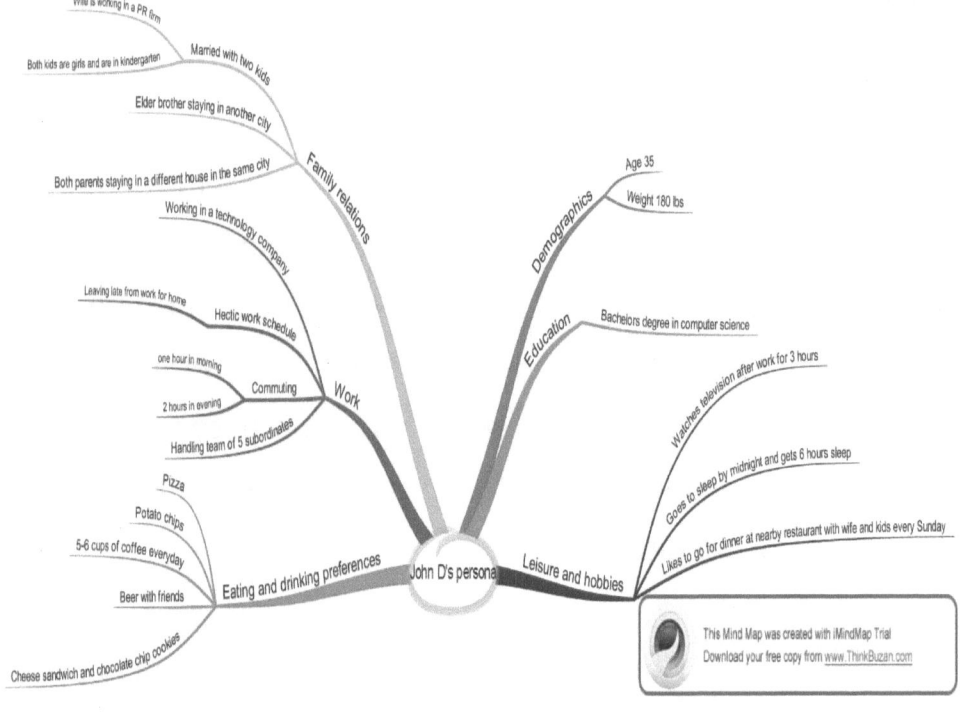

The above image is a sample mindmap that was created with the free version of iMindMap 11 software. This mindmap describes the persona of our case study character John D. The central theme or idea is John D's persona which is placed at the center of the mindmap. Different branches such as demographics, education, work, leisure and hobbies etc. describe various aspects of John D's persona.

Each of these branches also comprise of secondary branches that describe other attributes. When we consider John's individual transformation challenge of reducing obesity and improving fitness levels, we understand from the mindmap that John's eating and drinking preferences are unhealthy. Similarly, we can also infer that John's leisurely or hobby related activities does not contribute much in improving his fitness levels.

Thus, a mindmap can provide us with a snapshot of various dynamics that shape our overall personality and behavior patterns. This mindmap can help us to understand as to how our entrenched preferences as well as immediate environment might play a role in achieving our individual transformation goals.

We can determine the extent of detail that we intend to showcase in our mindmap. Greater detail will enable us to detect the subtle factors that may not seem too significant in itself but may eventually play a major role towards achieving the individual transformation goals.

For instance, one of the secondary branches in the work branch of the mindmap mentioned above describes that John handles a team of five subordinates. Maybe better training and delegation to these subordinates could free up more time for John, who in turn can then be able to leave from work on time. Thus, he may have more time after work to focus on improving his fitness levels. Thus, training subordinates may initially seem unrelated to achieving fitness goals but it eventually could play a major role towards accomplishing the individual transformation goals.

2. Persona Journey Map

Customer journey map is one of the main tools used in business process design to understand the customer experience while interacting with a product or a service. Customer journey map helps us to understand the different stages that a customer goes through while using a product or a service.

The customer journey map can also comprise of touchpoints that describe the key points at which the customer experiences the brand. Emotions experienced by the customer during various stages can also be highlighted in the customer journey map.

Customer journey map helps us to understand the emotional highs or lows that a customer faces during his experience with a brand. This journey map also helps us to understand the various pain points that a customer might face during his interaction with a brand. These pain points reduce the overall customer satisfaction level with respect to a product or a service.

Like we saw in case of persona mindmap, a persona journey map is a derivation of the customer journey map. While a customer journey map describes the customer experience with a product or a service in a great detail, persona journey map retains the focus solely on the individual. Persona journey map describes in detail a single experience that the individual has towards reaching a state or an outcome.

For example, if the main outcome of John D is obesity and poor fitness levels, then John goes through various experiences that play a role in shaping this outcome. For example, John might face a hectic work schedule on an average which drains him of any energy to pursue other hobbies or to achieve fitness related tasks such as going to gym after work. Similarly, the hectic work schedule compels John to sit in front of the television for several hours after work and also to go for unhealthy diet such as pizzas. We can create a persona journey map that describes John's experience from the moment he returns home after work.

As we observed how John's post work experience unfolded because of his hectic work schedule, our

HOW MIGHT I?

attention now shifts towards the work schedule itself. Our next question is how John allowed his work schedule to become so hectic that his leisure hours are also affected.

To address this question, we can create another persona journey map that describes his work schedule itself in detail. In this way, we can map out the various dynamics or forces that form the sum total of an individual's experience towards reaching an outcome.

The above diagram is a persona journey map that describes the persona journey of John D from leaving for work to returning home from work. This persona journey map was created with the free version of online brainstorming tool called as Mural.

The persona journey map comprises of five rows describing stages, steps, feelings, pain points and opportunities. Stages describe the broad phases of the overall journey. In case of John, stages include getting ready for work, commuting to work, starting work, lunch and socializing and so on.

Steps describe the exact activities that are a part of any stage. For example, getting ready for work stage may include steps such as freshen up and have breakfast, read newspaper, check messages on phone and so on.

Feelings describe the positive or negative feelings that may emerge in any stage. For example, in the commuting to work stage, John experiences positive feelings resulting from listening to good music on the radio. However, John also experiences negative feelings in this stage because of his frustration with waiting for traffic jam to clear up.

Pain points identify areas of improvement in any stage. Pain points determine the key factors that may hinder, interrupt, delay or distract an individual from completing a stage in the overall journey.

For example, constantly checking and responding to emails during work day is an interruption for John and is hence a pain point that needs to be addressed. In case of pain points, they may not only be obstructing the completion of any stage in the persona journey map but may also be the key towards achieving key objectives of an individual transformation exercise.

Thus, need to plan for new work items for next day instead of staying late in evening may not only help John to leave from work on time but also enable him to find more time after work to focus on his fitness goals. Hence, addressing this pain point in the post lunch work stage also significantly helps John towards achieving key objectives of the individual transformation exercise.

The last row in the persona journey map indicates opportunities. Opportunities row can be used to highlight the ways by which we can resolve the pain points mentioned earlier. We can highlight our ideas towards areas of improvement in each of the stage of the persona journey map in the opportunities space.

We can draw more than one persona journey maps in this step of the 5S-ITE process. A single persona journey map describes one event in detail. Similarly, we can create persona journey maps to describe other events in great detail.

For example, we can create a separate persona journey map to describe our case study character John's activities before he leaves for work. Similarly, we can also create another persona journey map to describe John's schedule or tasks once he reaches home from work.

In this way, we can determine stages, steps, feelings, pain points and opportunities for various events of an individual through the respective persona journey maps. Journey maps for different events will enable us to gather a rich repository of data that we can use to extract patterns and insights for the subsequent stages of the 5S-ITE process.

3. Focus Areas

Focus areas identifies the key themes that emerged from the analysis of persona mindmap and persona journey map. The ideas that emerge from the first two stages i.e. persona mindmap and the persona journey map of the 5S-ITE process helps us to detect the crucial areas for which need to identify the key goals as well as to develop the tasks for the subsequent stage. Accomplishing these tasks towards fulfilling the goals will also enable us to complete the individual transformation exercise.

Focus areas need not be more than four or five points that we can note down in a simple list. We can keep this list next to our persona mind maps and journey maps for quick reference. When we consider persona mindmap for analysis, we can check every single branch for its possible relevance to our individual transformation goals.

For example, in case of John, the leisure and hobbies as well as the eating and drinking preferences branches in the persona mindmap directly relate to his individual transformation goal of reducing obesity. However, the work branch may also play an important role in this exercise because his work schedule determines the time that John has for working on his fitness goals. Similarly, his nature of work might also be determining his eating and drinking preferences.

We can similarly analyze the persona journey map to figure out the specific stages and steps that are crucial towards accomplishing key goals of the individual transformation exercise. We can study each of the stages and steps in a persona journey map for a specific event to understand the important pain points and opportunities.

For example, John can improve the way he spends time before leaving for work. He also needs to focus on his tendency to accept new work items at the end of the work day, thereby staying late before leaving for home. Thus, we can list out the focus areas for John in the form of a simple list as follows:

1. Eating and drinking preferences
2. Leisure and hobbies
3. Activities or schedule before leaving for work
4. Leaving for home from work on time

We can now use this focus area list to compile a set of tasks for each focus area in the subsequent stage of the 5S-ITE process.

4. Task List

We can now further elaborate on the focus areas that we identified in the earlier step. We can now create detailed tasks for each of the focus area. We can also specify the duration for which need to perform these tasks.

We can use paper and pen to note down the tasks for the respective focus areas or we can also use a word document or a spreadsheet on a computer for this purpose. Task list can be a simple list with individual focus area as the main heading and the task name as the secondary heading. We can mention the duration, for which need to perform the task, below the task name.

Finally, we can include a heading for comments where we can mention details such as the task completion status, description about any interruptions or distractions to the task, number of days for which the task was performed at a stretch and so on.

We can also choose one or two focus areas and compile tasks for the same if we intend to test our overall schedule and pace. Subsequently, we can increase or decrease focus areas along with the respective tasks in order to sustain our momentum and to keep up with the objective of completing tasks on a daily basis.

The key to determine the number of focus areas and the respective tasks is to overcome the constraints that we saw earlier. In other words, we must choose the number of focus areas and create tasks for the same in such a way that we maintain our energy, retain our high morale and sustain our inner momentum towards completing the tasks on a daily basis. We would be able to achieve significant objectives of our individual transformation exercise if we are able to ensure sustained completion of tasks on a daily basis for any focus area.

Following is a sample task list for couple of focus areas for John:

Eating and Drinking preferences

Task: Eat fruit salad for breakfast

Duration: 30 days

Comments: Had a fruit salad breakfast for 15 days. Ate refrigerated pizza and cookies for breakfast on day 16 which was a Sunday

Task: Eat vegetarian food for lunch at work

Duration: 21 days

Comments: Had a vegetarian lunch at work for 21 days. Task completed successfully. Refrained from having heavy lunch on day 12 when senior manager was giving a party for the whole team.

Activities or schedule before leaving for work
Task: Perform simple exercise in the morning daily for 15 minutes
Duration: 30 days
Comments: Exercised for 15 minutes in the morning for 10 days at a stretch. Woke up late on day 11 which was a Sunday and then skipped exercise.

In this way, we can define tasks for focus areas and track their status on a regular basis. We can mention our observations along with task status in the comments section for the respective task.

5. Feedback

The 5S-ITE process culminates with the step called feedback. Feedback enables us to check the extent to which we have been able to achieve our overall individual transformation goals. The primary purpose behind creating persona mind maps, persona journey maps, defining focus areas and creating task lists is to accomplish a key individual transformation objective.

This overall individual objective must be considered once the previous four steps of the 5S-ITE process is completed. Thus, if we have completed one or two focus areas along with the respective tasks associated with them, we can then check the extent to which we have accomplished our individual transformation goals so far.

Thus, if reducing obesity is the individual transformation goal for John D as well as eating and drinking preferences is one of his key focus areas, then he can check his weight and fitness levels once he completes his tasks of having organic breakfast and lunch for 30 days. Feedback will guide us in checking the relevance of focus areas defined so far as well as the effectiveness of tasks belonging to these focus areas.

Hence, we can use insights obtained from feedback for doing course correction during the individual transformation exercise. We can use information obtained from feedback along with data available from the previous stages of the 5S-ITE process to make changes or add new focus areas or task lists.

It is natural to miss the forest for trees while working with focus areas and task lists. Feedback brings our attention back to the primary goal of individual transformation exercise. Feedback brings flexibility to the entire 5S-ITE process by enabling change or modifications depending upon what works well towards achieving the overall objective.

Feedback can be a simple statement describing the progress towards completing the individual transformation exercise.

Feedback can also include facts describing the extent to which focus areas and the respective tasks were completed in the specified time duration. You can

HOW MIGHT I?

subsequently correlate the effectiveness of focus areas and task lists with the completion of individual transformation goals so far.

CONCLUSION

This short text is my humble attempt to understand the intricacies of design thinking and to apply its concepts for the purpose of achieving individual transformation. Design thinking is responsible for achieving remarkable innovation in organizations globally.

Similarly, we can use design thinking based principles to understand and work around the various dynamics that interact with us in order to accomplish our individual transformation goals.

I identified the constraints of energy, morale and momentum at the outset because I believe that we must acknowledge the fact that we have limited cognitive resources at our disposal and that we must use this insight towards designing a unique and effective program towards achieving our individual transformation goals.

The five stages of the 5S-ITE process are relatively simple in the form of Persona mind maps, persona journey maps, focus areas, task lists and feedback. We can obtain rich data or insights in each of these stages depending upon the extent and depth of our analysis. 5S-ITE process is flexible and provides ample scope for course correction at any stage. I hope that this short text will inspire you to obtain deeper understanding of self and work towards achieving a lasting individual transformation. Good luck !

www.ingramcontent.com/pod-product-compliance
Lightning Source LLC
Chambersburg PA
CBHW030736180526
45157CB00008BA/3189